The Spy's Guide to Disguise

BY
A.M.Vale

WITH
H.KeithMelton
SPY EXPERT

SCHOLASTIC INC.

NEW YORK   TORONTO   LONDON   AUCKLAND   SYDNEY
MEXICO CITY   NEW DELHI   HONG KONG   BUENOS AIRES

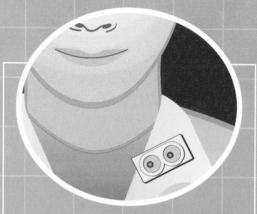

**Is this spy working undercover?
Turn to page 42 to find out!**

Turn to page 42 to find out!

ISBN 0-439-33644-9

Copyright © 2003 by Scholastic Inc.

Editor: Andrea Menotti
Designers: Robert Rath, Lee Kaplan, Marguerite Oerlemans
Illustrations: Daniel Aycock

Photos:
Page 25 (center), Library of Congress; page 25 (right), Mary Evans Picture Library;
page 41 (left), Princeton University Library. All other photos: ▬▬▬▬▬▬▬

12 11 10 9 8 7 6   5 6 7 8/0

Printed in the U.S.A.

First Scholastic printing, February 2003

The publisher has made every effort to ensure that the activities in this book are safe when done as instructed. Children are encouraged to do their spy activities with willing friends and family members and to respect others' right to privacy. Adults should provide guidance and supervision whenever the activity requires.

TABLE OF Contents

 This means you'll use your Spy Gear in this activity.

 This means you can find a related activity on the Spy University web site.

Meet the

Here are two spies. They can look like this:

But they can also look like this:

▼ Or this:

● WELCOME TO THE WORLD OF DISGUISE...

where you have as many possibilities as you see on this page, and then some! That's right—when you know the secrets of disguise, you can be your own creation, your own work of art, your own *masterpiece*, if you do say so yourself!

But that's all for later. For now, let's introduce you to the basics of disguise by answering two simple questions.

▼ Or this, this, this, and this:

NEW YOU (again and again and again!

WHY DO SPIES USE DISGUISES?

There are three main reasons:

● **To avoid surveillance.** To be successful in their work, spies have to avoid the watchful eyes of **counterspies**. Disguises help spies stay out of sight long enough to make exchanges, to have meetings, or to sneak into places where they're not supposed to be.

● **To escape.** If a spy needs to make a speedy getaway, a quick change of appearance can shake a counterspy off his tail.

● **To keep the spy's real identity a secret.** When meeting new contacts, a spy might use a disguise to cover up her features. That way, if the contact isn't trustworthy, the spy's true identity won't be exposed, and she won't be recognizable later.

WHAT KINDS OF DISGUISES ARE THERE?

First of all, there are **physical disguises**. That's when the features of your face or your body are changed or covered up. The type of physical disguise you use depends on your goal. Here are a few types:

■ **The quick change.** Remember this from your *Trainee Handbook*? It's when a spy quickly puts a yellow jacket over a blue shirt, removes a hat, or makes some other such change in order to give a pursuer the slip. You'll learn an advanced version of this technique in **Operation Super Spy** on page 35.

■ **The cover-up.** Examples of a cover-up include: a clown costume, a mask over your eyes, or a bandanna over your mouth. A less obvious type of cover-up disguise is a plain old pair of sunglasses (like the Spy Shades in this month's kit). If your goal is simply to be unrecognizable for a short time, then a cover-up will work fine. The only problem with obvious cover-ups is that people will *know* you're in disguise.

Must-haves for a Disguise Artist

Create a **disguise wardrobe**. Collect clothes unlike the kind you usually wear. This might involve looking for hand-me-downs from older siblings, or even your parents or grandparents. If the clothes are too big, you can:

- **Roll up shirtsleeves and pant cuffs.**
- **Wear extra padding.**
- **Use belts or suspenders.**
- **Stuff oversized shoes with handkerchiefs or extra socks.**

You should also look for interesting accessories to add to your disguise collection, like glasses, hats, and bags. If you can find a wig or two, even better!

If you *don't* want people to realize you're in disguise, and you want to be unrecognizable for a longer period, then you'll need a disguise that truly transforms you into someone else. We'll call that:

■ **The new you!** In this kind of disguise, you carefully change your appearance with makeup, a new hairstyle or hair color, false teeth, colored contact lenses, a change of wardrobe, and so on. The goal is to look like a whole different person. To make the transformation complete, the disguise might also involve changes in the ways you behave, move, sit, stand, and talk.

This brings us to the *ultimate* disguise: a total change of identity. When a spy takes on a false identity, it's called a **cover**. Spies develop covers to help them gain access to restricted places, or whenever it's not safe or convenient to be themselves. For example, when a spy wants to enter a country that has frosty relations with his own country, the spy might pretend to be a citizen of a more neutral country.

In order to pull this off, the spy will need a phony passport and plenty of other paperwork to back him up—like fake business cards, an address book with contacts in his "home country," cash in his wallet from that country, and so on. Of course, he'll also need to be pretty familiar with the customs and language of the country he claims to be from! All of this supporting information for the spy's cover identity is known as his **legend**.

PASSPORT

Ernest Cover
100 Legend Avenue
Anytown, AS 00007

In this guide to disguise, you'll learn all kinds of physical disguises, as well as the basic thinking that goes into creating covers and legends. So, get ready to meet the new you—over and over again!

ABOUT THIS MONTH'S SPY GEAR

This month, you've been issued a Disguise Kit that includes:

■ **Rearview Spy Shades.** They're great for hiding your eyes (one of your most recognizable features), and their rearview mirrors will let you watch what's going on behind you without having to turn your head!

Rearview Mirrors

■ **Spy Teeth.** Smile! You can hide your real dental features with this new set of extra-large chompers.

■ **Spy Face Pencils.** Use these pencils to draw moles, freckles, mustaches, and the wrinkles of old age!

■ **A Spy Signal Pin.** You can use your pin's color-changing eyes to send coded messages to your **spy network** when you're operating undercover.

■ **A Stick-on Mustache.** You can use this for a fun, quick disguise!

ABOUT THIS MONTH'S WEB SITE

the password spot

Shhhh. This month's web site password:

coverup

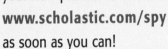

It's a disguise fest on the Spy University web site this month! First, you can help some spies get into disguise, then you'll take on a cover identity and see if you can keep your story straight when the heat is on! So, learn your new password and sneak on over to **www.scholastic.com/spy** as soon as you can!

This is the disguise kit of Antonio Mendez, the CIA disguise expert you'll be reading about in the Spy Feature on page 45. The kit includes makeup, a skin-tone color palette (to help in choosing the right skin tone for a disguise), hair coloring, fake hair, false teeth, false gums (called "lumpers"), and phony eyeglasses (without any magnification).

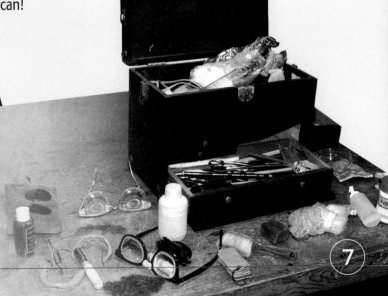

SPY TALK

▼ **Alias:** A false name a spy uses instead of his own.

▼ **Camouflage:** To disguise something by making it blend into its surroundings.

▼ **Code:** A system designed to hide the meaning of a message by substituting letters, numbers, words, symbols, sounds, or signals in place of the actual text.

▼ **Counterintelligence:** The protection of information, personnel, and equipment from spies.

▼ **Counterspy:** Someone who works in counterintelligence, investigating and catching spies.

▼ **Cover:** A false identity.

▼ **Dead drop:** A secret location used for exchange of material between a handler and a spy.

▼ **Detractor:** A feature (like a gold tooth or an obvious mole) that's added to a disguise to distract from other features (like a large nose). The "detractor" is memorable, while the other features of the spy's face are forgotten.

▼ **Exfiltrate:** To sneak someone out of a dangerous location.

▼ **Handler:** The intelligence officer who manages a spy's work.

▼ **Infiltrate:** To sneak into a hostile area.

▼ **Interrogate:** To question someone in detail.

▼ **Legend:** An artificial life history and background created to support a cover identity.

▼ **Lumpers:** False gums used to change a spy's jaw line.

▼ **Mole:** An employee of an intelligence service who secretly works for another country's intelligence service, or, generally speaking, a member of any group who's secretly loyal to a rival group.

▼ **Physical disguise:** A change or cover-up of bodily features.

▼ **Pocket litter:** The little items (like receipts, address books, and business cards) that a spy carries with him to support his cover identity.

▼ **Spy network:** A group of spies who work together toward a common goal.

▼ **Surveillance:** The careful study of someone or something.

See how simple disguises made this Russian mother and daughter look very different? They were members of the upper class who needed to escape Russia after the revolution of 1917. They disguised themselves as peasants so they could cross the Russian border undetected.

NORMAL APPEARANCE

IN DISGUISE

Spies
ON PARADE!

 It's Monday morning, and you're on your way into school when you're approached by Holly Minors and Tim Sharpe, two kids from the grade above you. They look really serious.

"We need your help," Holly says. "We're in charge of the float committee for this year's town festival parade, and we want to make sure that West Carson doesn't steal our ideas again."

"Remember last year?" Tim asks, looking grim.

"Oh, yeah," you say, thinking back to last year's parade, when the theme was "Back in Time," and West Carson, the school on the other side of town, had a float with a giant dinosaur on it, just like your school's—except West Carson's was

almost twice as tall and had flashing red eyes. It was pretty cool, you had to admit.

"And then the year before, we did a winter scene with fake snow, and so did they!" Holly says. "Coincidence? I don't *think* so."

"And they got first prize in the school category *both* years. It's *completely* unfair," Tim says. "We think they must have spies."

"We've heard you know about spy stuff," Holly says. "Is that true?"

"Sort of," you say, trying to be cautious about it.

"We were wondering if you'd be our spy," Tim says.

"You want *me* to find out what they're *building*?" you ask, appalled that Holly and Tim would even consider cheating like that.

"No!" Tim says quickly. "We just want to know if *they're* spying on *us*."

"Oh," you say, relieved.

"Do you think you can help us?" Holly asks.

"Sure, I'll see what I can find out," you say.

"Great," Tim says. "We're in the final phase of construction, so we'll be meeting every day this week on the playground near the parking lot. You'll come by?"

"Okay," you say.

As Tim and Holly leave, you start to think about your first step. The way you see it, you have two options. You could hang out at the float-building meetings at your school (East Carson) and keep track of any suspicious characters lingering around the area. You could even investigate the members of the committee—after all, there *could* be a mole in their midst.

Or, you could take the opposite approach and start off by visiting West Carson—in disguise, of course—so you could find out who's working on their float. This option is a lot riskier than the first one, because if you're discovered, you could be accused of spying for your school. But then again, it sure would be helpful to know who you're up against!

- ■ If you decide to start at your own school, turn to **page 18**.

- ■ If you decide to visit West Carson in disguise, turn to **page 22**.

This is your Spy Quest for this month. There's only one way to solve it, so choose your path wisely! If you hit a dead end, you'll have to back up and choose another path!

1

OPERATION Me First

Who are you? What makes you *you*? If you want to go into disguise, these are the first questions you have to ask yourself. There are lots of "ingredients" that go into *you*, and as a disguise artist, you have to know those ingredients inside and out. How do you look? How do you act? How do others describe and recognize you? This operation will help you find out. So, grab a friend, and let's get to know the real you!

STUFF YOU'LL NEED

- **Full-length mirror**
- **Pencil and paper**
- **Colored pencils, crayons, or markers**

YOUR NETWORK

- **A friend to share impressions of you**

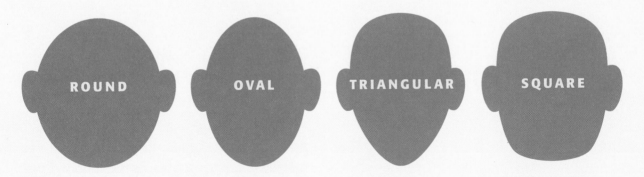

ROUND OVAL TRIANGULAR SQUARE

WHAT YOU DO

PART 1: HOW DO YOU LOOK?

First of all, you're going to make a self-portrait. It doesn't have to be perfect—so don't drive yourself nuts trying to get it exactly right. The main point is to get a basic idea of your physical features. It'll help to have a full-length mirror to consult as you draw.

1 We'll start with your face. The four common face shapes are drawn above. Which one is yours? Draw that shape to start your portrait.

2 Add your eyes. They should go halfway from the top of your head to your chin. As you draw them, think about their shape and arrangement. Are they close-set or wide-set? Big or small? And what about your eyebrows? Are they thick or thin? How are they shaped?

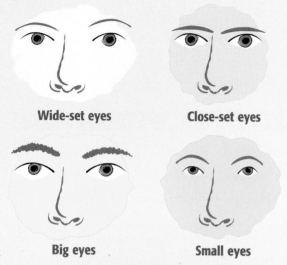

Wide-set eyes   Close-set eyes

Big eyes   Small eyes

3 Now draw your nose. Is it short or long? Thin or wide? Pointy? Turned up or straight? It's hard to show a nose from the front, so just do the best you can.

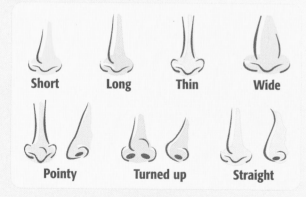

Short   Long   Thin   Wide

Pointy   Turned up   Straight

4 Draw your mouth. You don't have to draw yourself smiling. Just sketch the size and shape of your lips when your mouth is at rest.

5 Add your ears. For most people, the tops of their ears line up with the tops of their eyes, and the bottoms of their ears line up with the bottom of their nose. But you may have a different arrangement. Look in the mirror to check, and then draw your ears as you see them.

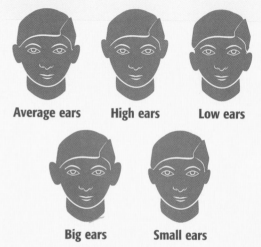

Average ears   High ears   Low ears

Big ears   Small ears

6 Sketch in your hair. If you wear your hair lots of different ways, choose the hairstyle you wear most often (or at least the one you've been wearing recently).

7 Draw your body. Use the mirror to see how long your neck is, how far your arms reach, and how long your legs are. Sketch your basic shape as well as you can.

8 Now add your wardrobe. Dress yourself in an outfit that you like to wear often. If you usually wear glasses, you should draw those, too. The same goes for jewelry.

9 Color yourself in! Use your colored pencils to match your eye color, hair color, and skin color.

10 If you have any identifying marks, like freckles, moles, or birthmarks, be sure to include those!

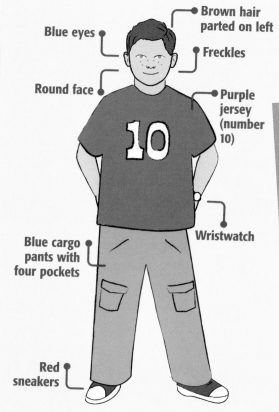

Brown hair parted on left

Blue eyes

Freckles

Round face

Purple jersey (number 10)

Blue cargo pants with four pockets

Wristwatch

Red sneakers

PART 2: HOW DO YOU ACT?

On another sheet of paper, answer the following questions. They'll help you take a close-up look at your personality and the ways you usually act.

1 Look at the list of personality traits on the right. For each one of them, decide if you act that way **often**, **sometimes**, **rarely**, or **never**.

2 Choose three words that *most* describe your personality. They can come from the list on the right, or they can be words you think up yourself.

3 What little habits or mannerisms do you have? Do you play with your hair? Bite your fingernails? Tap your feet? List anything you can think of.

4 How do you talk? Is your voice low or high? Do you tend to speak fast or slowly? Do you have an accent? Are there any expressions or words you often use (like "like," for example)? Do you gesture a lot when you talk? How?

	Often	Sometimes	Rarely	Never
Cheerful	☐	☐	☐	☐
Serious	☐	☐	☐	☐
Gloomy	☐	☐	☐	☐
Secretive	☐	☐	☐	☐
Talkative	☐	☐	☐	☐
Energetic	☐	☐	☐	☐
Nervous	☐	☐	☐	☐
Easygoing	☐	☐	☐	☐
Shy	☐	☐	☐	☐
Quiet	☐	☐	☐	☐
Outgoing	☐	☐	☐	☐
Independent	☐	☐	☐	☐
Loud	☐	☐	☐	☐
Neat	☐	☐	☐	☐
Organized	☐	☐	☐	☐
Calm	☐	☐	☐	☐
Daydreamy	☐	☐	☐	☐
Patient	☐	☐	☐	☐
Restless	☐	☐	☐	☐
Tough	☐	☐	☐	☐
Timid	☐	☐	☐	☐
Stern	☐	☐	☐	☐
Angry	☐	☐	☐	☐
Bold	☐	☐	☐	☐
Gentle	☐	☐	☐	☐

5 What's your posture like? Do you slouch or stand tall? Do you hunch your shoulders? Look down a lot?

6 How do you walk? Do you drag your feet? Do you normally walk briskly or stroll slowly?

PART 3: THE VIEW FROM OUTSIDE

Now that you've sketched yourself and answered some questions about the way you behave, it's time to find out how others see you.

1 Ask a friend to draw your picture, following the steps in Part 1. Here's the catch, though—your friend has to draw your portrait from *memory*. Don't let your friend look at your self-portrait, any photos of you, or the actual you!

2 Compare your friend's portrait to yours. What differences do you notice? What kinds of details did your friend include? Which details were left out? What about your hairstyle and clothes—do they look right to you? Ask your friend to explain anything that seems different from your own impression of yourself.

3 Now have your friend describe how you come across by filling out the questionnaire in Part 2 (about *you*).

4 Compare your friend's answers to yours. Does your friend see you as you see yourself? Did your friend point out anything new to you?

MORE FROM HEADQUARTERS

Now it's your friend's turn to go under the microscope! Have your friend draw a self-portrait and fill out the questionnaire, and then see how well you can draw and describe your friend. Do your impressions match up to your friend's self-description?

WHAT'S THE SECRET?

If you want to be a master of disguise, you need to get a good idea of how other people experience you. Your friend's impressions were probably similar in many ways to your own ideas about yourself, but pay attention to the differences. Maybe there were things your friend pointed out that you didn't realize about yourself, or maybe your friend didn't notice something about you that you thought was a big deal. You might find it interesting to repeat Part 3 with more friends. See if your friends have similar observations about you.

Once you're aware of how you present yourself, then *you're* in control. You know what people recognize about you, so you can change those things. So, get ready to slip into disguise....

(continued from page 18)

You follow Jacob home. It takes him long enough, but sure enough, he ends up going inside a house on Delancey Drive. There's a girl next door playing on her front lawn, so you decide to ask her about Jacob. Sure enough, she confirms that Jacob is not a West Carson student. *And* she tells you that Jacob's family just moved here a few months ago, so *that* explains why he didn't know about the town festival parade.

■ Oh, well. That was a dead end. Try another path!

OPERATION ABOUT Face

#2

If you could disguise only *one* part of your body, what would it be? Your elbow? Your left foot? Doubt it! If you *really* wanted to avoid being recognized, you'd focus on your face. So that's what this first disguise operation is all about! You'll learn how to disguise the structure of your face and the look of your teeth—and we'll throw in a few moles and freckles, too! So, if you're ready to *face* the new you, read on!

STUFF YOU'LL NEED

- **Blush (powder-style)**
- **Mirror**
- **Comb or brush**
- **Hair gel (optional)**
- 👓 **Spy Teeth**
- **Tissue**
- 👓 **Spy Face pencils**
- 👓 **Fake mustache**

YOUR NETWORK

- **A female senior spy to loan you some blush**

WHAT YOU DO

PART 1: SHAPES AND STYLES

In the first operation, you identified your face shape: round, oval, triangular, or square (turn back to page 11 if you don't know what this is all about!). Now you're going to disguise your face shape with some clever illusions! Just borrow some blush from a female senior spy—and if you're a boy spy, don't get hung up on the makeup part. Makeup is *not* just for girls; it's a spy tool, too!

1 If you have a round, square, or triangular face, you can make your face narrower by applying blush in vertical strokes on the sides of your face. Look in a mirror so you can see what you're doing, and brush the powder from your chin all the way up to your temples. Brush up and down until the sides of your face are noticeably darker than the front of your face. This creates the impression that your face is oval-shaped.

Round face made up to look narrower

2 If you have an oval face, you can make your face appear wider by applying blush in a horizontal direction on your cheek-bones. Shade as close to your hairline as you can get. This emphasizes the width of your face.

Note: Don't overdo it with the blush, or you might look feverish (or sunburned, or just plain weird!).

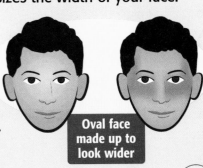
Oval face made up to look wider

3 Since your hair creates a frame around your face, you can also make the shape of your face look different

by changing your hairstyle. If you have a narrow (oval-shaped) face, comb your hair away from your face to give your face as much width as possible.

4 If you have a wide face (round or square), you can comb your hair forward to cover the sides of your face, or you can brush your hair back if it hangs down over your forehead. This will emphasize the length of your face.

5 Really, any change in your hairstyle will help disguise you, so try lots of different options! If you part your hair, try parting it on a different side than usual. If you usually comb your hair forward, comb it back (and vice versa). You could even try using hair gel to sculpt your hair into different styles.

PART 2: BIG MOUTH

Now it's time to swap your pearly whites for some…stainy yellows? And we'll show you how to change your jaw line, too. So, open wide!

1 Your Spy Teeth sure don't look like they've been to the dentist recently, do they? But rest assured, no matter how dirty they look, they were made fresh for you at Spy U's disguise department. So, open your mouth and stick your Spy Teeth inside. Bite down and smile! How do you like your new disguise?

2 If you want to make your jaw look bigger and fatter, you can stick a tiny piece of wet tissue under your lower lip, beneath your bottom teeth. Notice how this makes your lower lip stick out. Spies use jaw inserts like this (called **lumpers**) to change their profiles.

PART 3: LITTLE EXTRAS

If you want to add some distracting details to your face disguise, use your Spy Face pencils to create moles and freckles. These are identifying marks that people might notice and remember later when they describe you. ("He had a big mole right above his lip….")

1 Use your black Spy Face pencil to draw a mole somewhere on your cheek or above your lip. Don't overdo it—just a small spot will do.

2 If you don't already have freckles, use your brown Spy Face pencil to add dots on your nose and cheeks.

MORE FROM HEADQUARTERS

1 Here are some more little extras you can add to your face disguise:

■ Try putting on the fake mustache in this month's Spy Gear kit. How does that make you look? If you're a girl, could you be convincing disguised as a young man? You can also try drawing on a mustache with your brown or black Spy Face pencil.

■ Shade the area underneath your eyes so it looks like you haven't had enough sleep. To shade with your black Spy Face pencil, make lines and then rub them in with your fingertip.

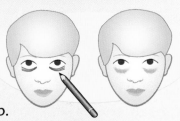

■ Put a small Band-Aid on your face. The Band-Aid will distract from your other features, especially if it is colored or has a pattern and you put it in a very visible spot.

2 Visit the Spy University web site (www.scholastic.com/spy) and disguise some spies! See how different you can make them look with new hairstyles, mustaches, beards, and clothes!

WHAT'S THE SECRET?

If you thought makeup was just for looking pretty (or scary on Halloween), think again. Spies know that the clever, careful use of makeup can really make people look different. Female spies have it easy, because it's normal for women to wear cosmetics, but guy spies have to make sure their makeup is hard to detect and rub off.

Changing your hairstyle is an easy way to disguise yourself, and male spies (the grown-up kind) have lots of options in that department, since they can change their facial hair, too. If you've ever seen the same man with and without a beard or mustache, you know what a difference those features can make. Beards, in particular, can really change the shape of a man's face.

This is the raw material for a fake mustache. It's real human hair attached to a thin lace backing. The disguise artist cuts the hair to the desired shape and glues it onto his face. The lace is so fine that it becomes invisible once it's glued to the skin.

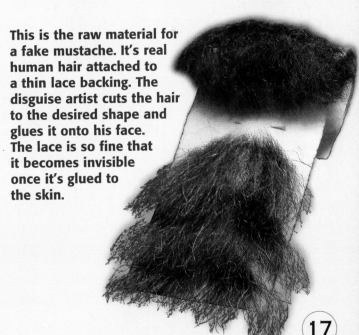

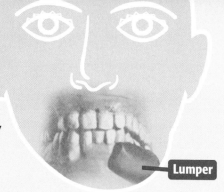

These models show how mouth inserts called "lumpers" can disguise a spy's jaw line.

Lumper

Lumper

Even little details like moles, freckles, Band-Aids, and stained, crooked, or gold teeth can play a key role in disguise. They're called **detractors**, because, if they're distracting enough, they'll *detract* (or draw people's attention away) from your other features. That means people will remember the detractor more readily than your real features.

Maybe you've noticed that there's one very important part of your face that we haven't touched upon yet. In fact, of all the parts of your face, people *focus on* this part (or should we say "these parts") the most. That's right—your eyes! Don't worry, we've got them covered, too. Just look over at the next operation, and you'll *see!*

(continued from page 10)

Y ou decide to pay a visit to your school's float construction meeting today after school. You arrive with your notebook to find Tim, Holly, two teachers, and about ten other kids hammering, cutting, gluing, and painting the various parts of the float.

Holly comes over to greet you, and you take the opportunity to ask her about any possible moles in the committee.

"Oh, no," she says. "Everyone here is working way too hard. No one would ever sabotage our chances like that."

"But still, someone *could* have other loyalties," you say.

"No, it couldn't be one of us," Holly says. "The ideas were leaking out last year and the year before, and everyone's new this year, except for me and Tim. I really think the threat's from outside. I mean, we're totally exposed here—we have to build the float out in the open 'cause we can't fit this huge thing

inside, and just look at all these people walking by. I bet one of them's from West Carson."

You decide Holly's probably right, so you spend the rest of the meeting watching the people who walk past. You see a woman pushing a baby carriage, a couple of teachers leaving for the day, a little old lady hunched over her loaded pushcart, and a boy about your age dribbling a basketball toward the playground. The boy stops when he sees the construction going on and watches with interest.

You decide to approach the boy and introduce yourself. He tells you his name is Jacob, that he goes to a private school nearby, and that he lives on Delancey Drive, which is just up the road from the school.

"What are you building?" Jacob asks.

"Can't you guess?" you ask.

"No," he says. "What is it?"

You look him straight in the eye to see if he's playing dumb.

"It's a parade float," you say.

"Oh," he says innocently. "For what parade?"

You tell him, and soon he's off on his way. You really wonder, though, how this kid could not know about the town festival parade. Everyone knows about it—it's one of the biggest events the town has. Maybe this is worth investigating? Or maybe you'd better stay focused on the bigger picture and go to West Carson tomorrow to see what's going on over there.

■ If you decide to follow Jacob home to check out his story, turn to **page 14**.

■ If you decide to go to West Carson tomorrow (in disguise), turn to **page 22**.

OPERATION Eye: CAN'T SEE YOU

There's a lot to the old saying, "The eyes are the windows to the soul." Your eyes reveal a lot of information about who you are, how you're feeling, and what you're thinking. Other people's eyes will naturally lock onto yours as they try to recognize you and figure you out. That's why, if you want to avoid being recognized, you should put some Spy Shades over those windows to your soul, as this operation will show you.

STUFF YOU'LL NEED

- Any or all of the disguise supplies you used in **Operation About Face**
- **Clothes unlike the kind you normally wear**
- **Spy Shades**

YOUR NETWORK

- **Some friends to not recognize you**

WHAT YOU DO

First of all, it's got to be a sunny day if you're going to look normal in your Spy Shades, so if it's dreary and gray outside, try another operation! But if the sun's out and the skies are clear, then you're *clear* to continue!

1 Disguise yourself as described in **Operation About Face**: Change your face shape, restyle your hair, add your Spy Teeth, and draw on a mole or some freckles, if you want.

2 Put on clothes that you don't ordinarily wear. Try for a completely different look. If you normally go for casual sweats and sneakers, for example, then put on something snazzy or dressy. Won't your mother be happy!

3 Then put on your Spy Shades. Now that your eyes are covered, people won't be able to make eye contact with you. Better yet, since your Spy Shades are equipped with rearview mirrors, you can look at people with your back to them, without revealing your face at all.

4 Set up a meeting with a friend in a crowded and safe place, like a park or a school playground.

5 Go to the meeting in your disguise, and walk right past your friend, trying to blend into the crowd. When you pass, **do not look** in your friend's direction. Try to look natural. Pretend that you really *are* someone else entirely, on a normal walk in the park. Does your friend recognize you? Check in your rearview mirrors to see if your friend turns as you pass.

6 Stand with your back to your friend a short distance away, and use your rearview mirrors to watch as your friend looks for you. How long does your disguise hold up?

7 If your friend recognizes you, ask what gave you away. If your friend *doesn't* recognize you, then congratulations—mission accomplished!

8 Try this same exercise with other friends. If something gave you away before, change that aspect of your disguise this time. How many friends can you slip past?

MORE FROM HEADQUARTERS

For an extra challenge, try the exercise described above, but this time, don't wear your Spy Shades. Just don't *look* at your friend as you pass by. Look down, straight ahead, or to the side, and let yourself blend into the crowd. Can you avoid being noticed this way?

WHAT'S THE SECRET?

When you make eye contact with someone, you're inviting that person to notice you, to try to recognize you, and maybe even to communicate with you. That's why, when you *don't* want to be noticed or recognized, you avoid eye contact.

Your Spy Shades not only eliminate eye contact, but they cover a very recognizable part of your face. Celebrities try this trick all the time—you've probably seen pictures of movie stars wearing dark glasses out in public. In order for the trick to work, though, it has to be sunny outside, and you have to seem calm, cool, and relaxed—not nervous and suspicious!

(continued from page 22)

You put on your Spy Shades, load your quick change bag, plan a cover story (in which you're a student from another local school, not East or West Carson), and you make your way over to West Carson. You pass by their float-building meeting, using your rearview mirrors to sneak a peek at what's going on. You scan the faces of the float builders, and you even get a basic idea of the float they're building. It's too soon to tell, but their float *does* seem to have great big trees on it—like your school's rain-forest float. You're just about to turn around and make another pass when you hear:

"Hey, aren't you from East Carson?"

Uh-oh. Better think fast.

■ If you decide to go with the cover story you planned, turn to **page 40**.

■ If you decide to just say no and walk off as fast as you can (and make a quick change if you're followed), turn to **page 36**.

OPERATION
BODY
Builder

People come in lots of different shapes and sizes, and so can you! It's easy to disguise your shape by making it bigger (making it *smaller* is another story!). If someone meets you for the first time when you're disguised as a heavy-set person, he'll have that image of you in his mind—and he'll have a tough time recognizing you once you've shed your extra bulk (which, in this case, is pillows, scarves, and towels!). So, try this operation, and you'll get the *big* idea!

STUFF YOU'LL NEED

- **Scarves**
- **Towels (large and small)**
- **Safety pins**
- **Big pants**
- **Pillows**
- **String**
- **Big overcoat (ankle-length)**
- **Hat**
- **Spy Shades**

YOUR NETWORK

- **A friend to help you get into disguise**
- **More friends to fool with your disguise**

WHAT YOU DO

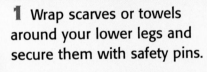

1 Wrap scarves or towels around your lower legs and secure them with safety pins.

2 Put on your big pants. Your wrapped-up calves should fill them up nicely.

3 Wrap scarves or towels around your upper arms and secure them with safety pins, too.

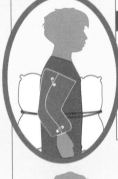

4 Now put one pillow on your stomach and another one on your back (so you're sandwiched between two pillows). Have your friend help you secure them by tying one or two strings around your middle (not too tight!).

5 Place a towel across your shoulders and wrap a scarf around your neck.

6 Now put on your overcoat. Button it up to make sure your front pillow isn't visible!

7 Practice walking like someone who's carrying around a lot of extra weight. Lean back and stick your stomach out. Walk more slowly than usual, wobble and waddle, and seem like you're out of breath!

8 Now put on your hat and your Spy Shades, go outside, and walk by people you know. Do they realize it's you? If not, how long does it take them to catch on (if at all)?

MORE FROM HEADQUARTERS

Add a little makeup to your disguise. A very heavy-set person will often have a reddish face (especially after exercise), so put some blush on your cheeks.

WHAT'S THE SECRET?

This disguise is designed to be worn outside in cold weather. You'll look very strange if you wear this getup inside or during the summer, so be wise about when and where you bulk up! Remember, if your goal is to *really* look like someone else (and not just to cover yourself up), then your disguise isn't doing its job if it calls attention to itself!

(continued from page 10 or 18)

You decide to plan a visit to West Carson. You start by calling West Carson's office (pretending to be a student there) and saying that you'd like to join the float building committee. The nice secretary tells you exactly when and where the meetings are.

Your next step is to plan your disguise. You consider a lot of options, but you like two of them best.

Your first option is to disguise yourself as an old lady. You have the perfect model for your disguise—that old lady you've seen sometimes walking past the school. She'd be easy to imitate,

since she's just about your height, and you know you have the items you'd need to create that disguise—a bulky old overcoat, a tattered hat, a gray wig, and even a little shopping cart like the one the old lady's always pushing. That cart would be a great place to store your spy stuff for easy access.

Your second option is to keep your physical disguise simple. You could just use your Spy Shades to cover up your eyes, and you could carry a quick change in case you're followed. You could also develop a cover identity to use in case

you're approached and questioned.

The only problem with the second option is that it's been kind of gray lately—not exactly sunglasses weather, so part of you wonders if your Spy Shades might look strange and call attention to you. But then again, if someone saw through your old lady disguise, it would be pretty tough to talk your way out of that one!

■ If you decide to disguise yourself as an old lady, turn to **page 28**.

■ If you decide to go with your Spy Shades, turn to **page 20**.

OPERATION GROW UP

It takes a long time to grow up, but if you want to add an inch or two to complete your spy disguise, you don't have to wait around for nature. There are a whole bunch of ways you can get taller just by the way you dress and stand. Try this operation to give yourself a quick boost!

STUFF YOU'LL NEED

- Long pants
- Shirt of the same color as your pants
- Two pairs of tube socks
- Big boots
- Hat

WHAT YOU DO

1 Put on the long pants and the shirt. You should be all the same color now.

2 Tuck in the shirt—this makes your legs look longer.

3 Roll each pair of tube socks together and put one pair of socks inside the heel of each boot.

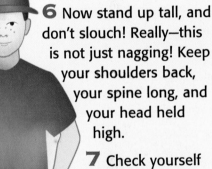

4 Step into the boots. You should feel yourself lift up at least an inch! Now lace up the boots, and fix your pant legs so they hang down over your boots.

5 Put on the hat. Don't push it down over your eyes, but let it sit on the top of your head.

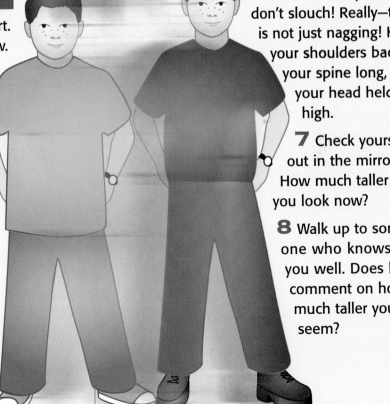

6 Now stand up tall, and don't slouch! Really—this is not just nagging! Keep your shoulders back, your spine long, and your head held high.

7 Check yourself out in the mirror. How much taller do you look now?

8 Walk up to someone who knows you well. Does he comment on how much taller you seem?

MORE FROM HEADQUARTERS

1 Try adding big shoulders to your tall-person disguise! Ask a female senior spy if you can borrow a jacket or a shirt that has shoulder pads. If that doesn't work out, then you can make your own shoulder pads by putting on a jacket and stuffing a rolled pair of socks into each shoulder. Do you feel like you're looming even bigger and taller now?

2 Check your closet for a pair of pants with vertical stripes. Try them on and look in the mirror. Do the vertical stripes make your legs look longer? They should!

WHAT'S THE SECRET?

Anything that creates a strong vertical line will make you seem taller. By wearing the same color on your top and bottom, you became one single vertical line. Wearing vertical stripes helps, too, since long stripes emphasize your length.

But the biggest thing you can do to look taller is to *feel* taller. Stand tall (or sit up straight), hold your head high, and really *believe* that you're bigger. It'll do wonders for your confidence (which every spy disguise requires!).

SPYquest

(continued from page 31)

You look directly at the old lady, and you see that her hair is obviously a wig. In one quick move, you pull the wig off. It's a boy in disguise!

"Who are *you*?" you ask.

The boy doesn't wait around to answer. He snatches his wig back and, in the tussle, he knocks over your pushcart. Your camera and notebook come tumbling out, and you both dive for them,

but the boy grabs them first and dashes off. You chase the boy as far as you can, but your beat-up shoes will hardly stay on your feet.

The next day, the consequences are grim. You're called down to the principal's office, and you find Holly, Tim, and your camera and notebook there. You try to explain that you're pretty sure the kid you encountered was a spy from

West Carson, but the principal just shakes his head, saying he's very disappointed that you chose to handle the problem this way instead of bringing it to his attention. As a result, your school's float will not be entered in the parade this year.

■ Ouch. That was a pretty harsh dead end. Turn back and choose another path!

CHEVALIER D'EON
A FRENCH SPY WITH A TWIST

Would you consider going into disguise as someone of the opposite gender? Do you think you could be convincing?

One French spy did just that. His name was (get ready for this—it's a mouthful!) Chevalier Charles Geneviève Louis Auguste André Timothée D'Eon de Beaumont, and he lived from 1728 to 1810. He was very intelligent, and he was great at fencing (jousting with swords). These talents brought him to the attention of France's King Louis XV, who had a spy network called *Le Secret du Roi* (The King's Secret). Louis wanted spies who were good thinkers and fighters, and D'Eon was a perfect candidate.

D'Eon agreed to become one of the king's agents, and he was sent on his first mission—to Russia—in 1756. His job was to help convince Russia's leader, Czarina Elizabeth Petrovna, to leave an alliance with France's enemy, England, and to ally Russia with France instead.

According to D'Eon's account, he succeeded in this mission, where all other French agents had failed, by posing as a woman! This allowed him to gain access to the czarina's inner circle and invitations to courtly masquerade balls (where, interestingly enough, the czarina liked to dress as a man!).

Once he'd won the czarina's trust, D'Eon was able to persuade her to enter into a correspondence with Louis XV, opening the door to warmer relations between the two countries.

Historians are not certain if D'Eon posed as a woman the entire time he was in Russia, or if the czarina was really fooled, but it's clear that he *did* dress in women's clothes at least on occasion, and he did succeed in winning over the czarina.

Unfortunately, though, the rest of D'Eon's life did not go as well as his first mission. He continued to dress in women's clothes, and controversy began to swirl over whether or not he really was a woman. By the time he died, there was so much fascination and speculation over his gender (people were even placing bets!) that an exam was done just to answer the question once and for all. As it turned out, he was most certainly male.

GoGray

6

Old people sure look innocent, don't they? And sometimes they're very small, too— so it wouldn't look completely out of the ordinary for a kid-sized spy to be wrinkly and gray-haired, would it? This operation will show you how to add seventy years to your face, so get ready to leap into the future—warp speed ahead!

STUFF YOU'LL NEED

- **Foundation (to match your skin tone)**
- **Spy Face pencils (brown and white)**
- **Baby powder**
- **Clothing that older people wear**
- **Eyeglasses (optional)**

YOUR NETWORK

- **A female senior spy to loan you some foundation**
- **A senior spy to remove lenses from a pair of glasses (optional)**

WHAT YOU DO

1 Dab the foundation on your face and rub it around until your face is evenly coated.

2 Now you're going to use your Spy Face pencils to emphasize the lines and grooves on your face (since this is what happens to your skin as you get older). First, use your brown Spy Face pencil to make "bags" under your eyes. Draw a few dark half-circles underneath each eye and rub them in.

3 Now squint, and darken the squint lines on the sides of your eyes. People call these "crow's feet."

4 Now shade the deep parts of your eyes and the sides of your nose. Start near the center of your eyelid and shade all the way down to your nostrils. Rub the pencil lines in.

5 Sketch in your forehead wrinkles. Raise your eyebrows as high as you can, and go over the horizontal lines on your forehead with your brown pencil.

6 Now you're going to add your frown lines. So, scowl as much as you can and darken the vertical lines on your forehead and the grooves around your mouth.

7 Time to pucker up! We're going to add your kiss lines, so pucker your lips like you're going to kiss someone, and sketch in the vertical lines around your mouth.

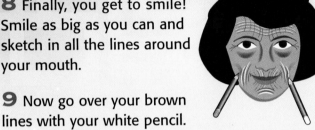

8 Finally, you get to smile! Smile as big as you can and sketch in all the lines around your mouth.

9 Now go over your brown lines with your white pencil. Anywhere you've added brown lines, add white lines beside them. Rub all the lines to blend them together.

10 If you're a girl, add some blush and some lipstick in colors you think an old lady might choose.

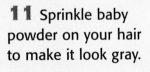

11 Sprinkle baby powder on your hair to make it look gray.

12 Now, without ruining your makeup, put on the kinds of clothes you've seen old people wear. Remember that old people usually choose their clothing for comfort, and they often wear styles from many years ago. If you're disguising yourself as an old lady, remember your accessories, too. You might add some jewelry, a hat with a veil, or an old-fashioned handbag.

13 If you want, ask a senior spy to help remove the lenses from some old eyeglasses (in a style old people might wear), and add those to your disguise as well.

MORE FROM HEADQUARTERS

1 Practice standing and walking like an old person. Remember old people usually move slowly and are sometimes unsteady. Brace yourself by holding onto handrails whenever they're available. You might even try using a cane!

2 Try to fool some friends with your old person disguise. See if you can walk right past them without being recognized!

SPYtales

Hollywood makeup artists helped American spies develop disguise methods during World War II (1939–1945). Back then, the American intelligence service was the OSS (Office of Strategic Services), the forefather of the CIA. The OSS created a manual of disguise techniques called the "Manual on Personal Disguise" with help from the research laboratories of Max Factor, one of Hollywood's biggest makeup manufacturers. The manual, which was thirty-three pages long, described techniques for changing skin color, adding height, and looking older. One of the aging methods involved applying a wrinkling cream that slowed the flow of blood to the face to make facial muscles sag!

WHAT'S THE SECRET?

Makeup can be used to create lots of illusions, as you've probably seen in the movies. In this operation, you're using makeup to mimic the effects of aging. It's the kind of illusion that works best when viewed from a distance, or when you only expect to be seen briefly. Spy disguise experts have special technical makeup and masks that can hold up under much closer inspection.

Here you can see the step-by-step process of aging a woman's face with makeup. The photos show half of her face with makeup and half without, so you can see the difference. The final photo shows the complete disguise.

 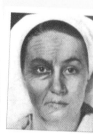 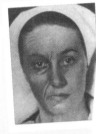 

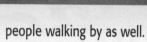
SPYquest

(continued from page 22)

You disguise yourself as an old lady, putting on the necessary makeup, then adding a bulky old overcoat, a wig, a hat, and a pair of your mother's old shoes from the garage. You also find an old shopping cart in your basement and load it with grocery bags full of stuff from the back of your pantry. In the top bag, you place a notebook and a pencil for your notes. You also decide to throw in your camera so you can take some pictures of West Carson's float-building committee.

Once you've completed your disguise, you make your way over to West Carson.

You locate the float-building meeting, and you walk by it slowly, trying to sneak a few glances. To your dismay, it looks like West Carson's float is similar to your school's rain-forest float in a lot of ways, though it's too soon to tell for sure. You try to pay the most attention to the people who are building the float. After you've passed by, you perch up on a hill above the school and make some sketches and notes about the people you've seen. You snap a quick picture, too, on your way back out. All goes well, and no one seems to even notice you're there, since there are plenty of other people walking by as well.

Then, as you're walking back toward your side of town, you're shocked to see two of your teachers, Mr. Shader and Ms. Lightly, heading right toward you. You're on the same sidewalk, so they'll pass you very closely. You panic—what if they see through your disguise? How would you ever explain why you were over near West Carson, dressed up as an old lady?

■ If you decide to turn the other way and get out of sight as fast as you can, turn to **page 34**.

■ If you decide to stay calm and keep walking right on by, turn to **page 31**.

7

OPERATION
Spy WALKER

The next time you're on a busy sidewalk, in a park, or in a shopping mall, have a look around and see how people walk. You'll probably notice that there are lots of different ways of walking. Some people might walk fast, while others might stroll slowly along. Some people take big strides; others take little, shuffling steps. There might be a few people with a little bounce in their step, and some with a lot of swing in their hips. But whatever you notice, one thing will be clear: Walking is no simple matter of one-foot-in-front-of-the-other! This operation will show you some of the many ways it can be done, so put on your walking shoes and step right this way....

STUFF YOU'LL NEED

- **Walking shoes (not open-toed)**
- **Pebble**
- **Ruler**
- **Two handkerchiefs or strings**
- **Long pants**

WHAT YOU DO

PART 1: FIND YOUR STRIDE

1 First, try walking very fast, but take small steps. How does it feel? Have you ever seen anyone walking this way?

2 Now try walking fast again, but this time take *big* strides. With each step, plant your heel out firmly in front of you. Keep your legs as straight as you can. Stand up tall, and let your arms swing freely. If you saw someone walking this way, what might you assume about her personality?

3 Now try walking super slow. Take small steps. In what kinds of situations do people walk this way?

4 Now try leaning back and walking slowly. Let your arms dangle loosely at your sides. You can also try clasping your hands behind you, or putting your hands in your pockets.

5 Now try leaning forward and walking slowly. Look down at the ground and let your shoulders sag. When do people walk like this? What if you wrapped your arms around your stomach—what might *that* say about you?

6 Now try swinging your hips from side to side as you walk. Really let 'em sway! What kinds of people walk like this?

7 Try putting a little bounce in your step. Each time you take a step, land on a bent leg and rise up to your tiptoes before you step onto your other foot. This will make you bob up and down as you walk. What would you think if you saw someone walking like this?

8 How about walking with your toes turned out or your toes turned in. What's that like?

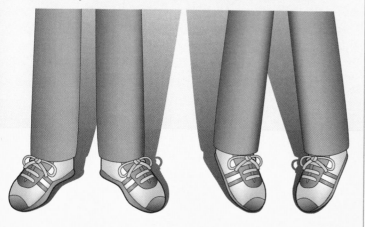

9 Try walking without lifting your feet up much at all. Have you seen people walking like this? What about lifting your feet up a *lot*? When do people walk like that?

10 Usually when you walk, you step onto your heel first, then you roll through to your toes. How about stepping onto your toes first, then putting your heel down? How does that feel? Try walking without putting your heels down at all. Why is that a quieter way of walking?

PART 2: LET'S LIMP

Now that you've tried lots of different ways of walking, let's try two different ways to disguise your walk with *injuries*—first by pretending to have a sore foot, then by faking a stiff knee.

● PEBBLE

1 To walk with a sore foot, take the pebble and put it in the heel of one of your shoes. This will help you remember that you're pretending to have a sore foot, *and* it'll remind you which foot is supposed to be in pain. After all, if you happen to sit down for a while, you wouldn't want to get up and start walking normally! Or, even worse, you wouldn't want to suddenly start limping on the wrong foot!

2 Now put on your shoes and start walking. Each time you step onto the "sore" foot (with the pebble), put very little weight on it and immediately step onto the other foot. As you stagger slowly along, be sure to wince a little as you try to bear the "pain!"

3 To walk with a stiff knee, take the ruler and use the handkerchiefs or strings to tie it to the back of one of your legs, behind your knee. Don't tie it too tight—we don't want any circulation loss at Spy University!

4 Put on your long pants to cover up the ruler.

5 Start to walk. The leg with the ruler tied to it will stay stiff, and you'll have to hoist it along with you. You'll have a rough time on stairs, so stay on level ground!

6 When using either of these "injured" walks as part of your spy disguise, be ready to explain how you hurt yourself if people ask!

MORE FROM HEADQUARTERS

1 Try on lots of different shoes, and see how they affect the way you walk. Try high heels, flip-flops, and boots that go all the way up to your calves. Try shoes that are too big for you, too. (You can stuff some socks in the toes so they fit.)

2 Have you ever tried walking with a cane? Try it! It'll be a great skill to add to your old person disguise (see **Operation Go Gray** on page 26).

WHAT'S THE SECRET?

The way you walk says a lot about you, and when you go into disguise, your walk and your posture need to fit the new you. Now that you've practiced walking all these different ways, you'll have a whole range of walking styles to choose from once you start to develop your cover identities (see **Operation Straight Story** on page 37 for more on this).

Being in control of your walk can also help you blend into your environment. If you're spying in an area where people are strolling casually along (like on a beachfront boardwalk or in a shopping mall), you don't want your walking style to make you stick out of the crowd. Even if you're very nervous or in a rush (because you're being pursued by **counterspies**!), if you can control your walk, you'll be able to **camouflage** yourself in the crowd!

RULER

HANKIES

SPYquest

(continued from page 28)

You walk by calmly and coolly, looking the other way, and Ms. Lightly and Mr. Shader don't even notice a thing, they're so busy talking to each other. Good move!

But then, a few minutes later, you look up, and coming right toward you is the very model for your disguise—that little old lady you've seen wandering around your school's grounds! And wow, she's approaching *fast*. Too fast. She must have taken some vitamins today! You brace yourself as she's about to pass you, hoping she doesn't see through your disguise and make a scene or something—but then, as she passes, you catch a glimpse of her hands on her pushcart's handle. Is it your imagination, or do those hands look really...young? Something tells you this is worth investigating.

- If you decide to take a risk and confront the old lady directly, turn to **page 24**.

- If you decide to follow the old lady, turn to **page 44**.

OPERATION Voice CHOICE

Chameleons are great role models for disguise artists, but when it comes to voice-changing, did you know that it helps to be like a parrot, too? Absolutely! Just like parrots mimic the voices they hear, you can change your voice by copying someone else's (with permission, of course!). You can also make your voice sound different by changing the shape of your mouth, pinching your nose, letting your tongue be lazy, or making other adjustments along those lines. So, if you're ready to have some choice when it comes to your voice, read on!

STUFF YOU'LL NEED

- Tape recorder
- Pencil

YOUR NETWORK

- Friends or family members who are willing to be mimicked
- Friends or family members to evaluate your results

WHAT YOU DO

PART 1: VOICE GYMNASTICS

There are lots of ways you can make your voice sound different just by making physical changes to your mouth and nose, and by pushing the limits of your natural voice. Try all these ways and record yourself so you can hear them later!

1 Go to a quiet place, sit down with your tape recorder, and press RECORD. First talk a little bit to get a sample of your natural voice (because even that will sound different to you when you play it back).

2 Now try pinching your nose while you talk. Can you make

your voice sound the same way *without* holding your nose? This is what people call a "nasal" voice.

3 Try puckering your lips and holding that shape while you talk. What do you notice about the way you sound?

4 Let your tongue sit lazily on the floor of your mouth as you speak. Which letters are hard to say that way? Say "hello." How does it sound?

5 Try pronouncing every single sound in every word you speak as crisply as you can. Exaggerate the movement of your lips as you speak, and say each word slowly.

6 Now try holding your lips very still as you speak. Which letters are hard to say like this? Try saying the words "peanut butter." How do they sound?

7 Try talking with a pencil clenched in your teeth. Say the words "extra special." What do you notice?

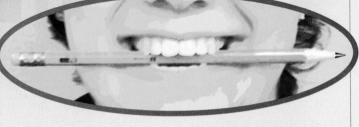

8 Try speaking as low as you can go. Then try speaking as high as you can. What's your range like? Is it easier for you to go higher or lower?

9 Speak super fast, and then try talking extra slow, like you're in slow motion.

10 Play back your vocal exercises. How do you sound? Which of these techniques created the most different-sounding voice? The most natural-sounding voice?

PART 2:
THE VOICE COLLECTOR

In this part of the operation, you'll collect some voice samples. Then you'll analyze the voices and do your best to reproduce them with your own vocal equipment!

1 Choose a friend or a relative who has a voice you want to imitate. For an extra challenge, see if you can find someone who has an accent that's a lot different from yours.

2 Now you're going to record a voice sample. Ask your friend or relative to tell you a story. It could just be the story of what happened to him that day, or it could be a story from long

ago. If your subject gets stage fright (or, in this case, *recorder* fright), ask some questions or start a conversation. As your subject talks, record your voice sample. You should record for about five minutes.

3 After you've finished recording, go to a quiet place and listen to the voice sample. Think through each of these questions:

- What do you notice about the tone of this person's voice? Is it high-pitched? Deep and low? Gravelly? Scratchy? Nasal (like when you pinch your nose)?

- What about the person's accent? Does it sound a lot different from yours? In what ways?

- Are there words that this person pronounces differently than you would?

- Does this person pronounce consonants (like B, D, P, and T) very crisply or softly?

- Does this person talk quickly or slowly?

- Does this person speak in long, winding phrases? Short and choppy ones?

- Are there any expressions that this person uses over and over again?

4 Play the recording again, but this time, try to imitate some phrases as you listen. Stop and rewind many times, so you can get lots of practice.

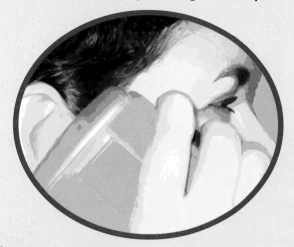

5 When you feel like you can imitate the voice pretty well, go find your friend or relative again, and perform his voice. Have another friend or relative listen to your imitation, compare it to the original, and give you feedback. Which voice qualities did you successfully imitate? Which ones do you need to work on?

6 Repeat steps 1 through 5 with another subject. See how many voices you can add to your collection!

MORE FROM HEADQUARTERS

Try some of the voice exercises you learned in Part 1 while you're on the phone with a friend. Ask your friend which ones sound the most real? The most unlike you?

WHAT'S THE SECRET?

You have a lot of control over your voice, and the more you listen to other voices and experiment with the range of your own, the more voice choices you'll have. You might be surprised to find how a simple change of voice (from soft and shrill to low and commanding, for example) can change the way people respond to you.

Spies will sometimes turn to voice disguises for phone conversations when they don't want to be recognized later.

Spies realize that once their voices have been recorded, they can later be traced. The NSA (the National Security Administration) has computer software that records phone conversations and makes "voice prints" (kind of like a fingerprint, except it's of your voice) of certain key words or phrases. Then when the NSA monitors telephone conversations, they can have their computers search to identify conversations that contain the same voice prints.

(continued from page 28)

You quickly turn around and walk back the way you came, but just when you think you're in the clear, you see a whole bunch of kids coming from West Carson's float-building meeting! You brace yourself, hoping they'll just ignore you, but no—one of them, a boy, actually seems to be approaching you!

"Wait a minute," the boy says, as he gets closer. "You're not…"

You panic and turn around, but there are Ms. Lightly and Mr. Shader.

"Hey!" the kids start shouting and chasing after you. One of them grabs your wig and your coat.

"I bet that's a spy from East Carson!" someone shouts.

"Spy!" the others shout.

"What's going on here?" Mr. Shader asks.

Well, guess what? It's over. You're exposed, and the consequences are stiff. When your principal finds out about it, your school's float is removed from the parade.

■ That was definitely a dead end. Turn back and try again!

Remember back in your *Trainee Handbook* when you learned how to do a quick change to disguise yourself? You just changed a jacket or a hat, and *poof*— you disappeared into a crowd! Well, you'll do the same thing here, except now you're going to change a lot more about you, using the skills you've learned so far in your disguise training. You'll be like Clark Kent disappearing into a phone booth and emerging as Superman (or in your case, Super *Spy*!).

STUFF YOU'LL NEED

- **Different clothes from the kind you usually wear**
- **Backpack**
- **Comb or brush**
- **Spy Shades**

YOUR NETWORK

- **A friend to not recognize you**

WHAT YOU DO

1 Load a quick change bag (otherwise known as your backpack) with some clothes that are very different from the kind you usually wear. Go for a completely different look. If you're normally really neat, choose a wrinkly shirt and big baggy pants (maybe even with stains or holes). Or, if you're not into sports, try a football jersey or a T-shirt with the name of a sports team on it. You'll also need a comb or a brush, and throw in your Spy Shades for good measure.

2 Choose a location where there are lots of people and a bathroom nearby where you can change (a locker room would also do). A good

FRIEND

choice would be your school, just after the school day ends.

3 When the school day ends, meet your friend and say you're going to run back inside to get something you forgot. Ask your friend to wait for you outside.

Here's the spy when he first meets his friend.

SPY

4 Go to the bathroom and make your quick change. Put on your new clothes and change your hairstyle by brushing it a different way. As a finishing touch, put on your Spy Shades.

5 Go back outside. As you come out, walk in a different way than you usually do— so if you normally walk fast with a bounce in your step, lean back and stroll slowly, for example. Look casual, and *don't* look at your friend. Try to just blend into the crowd. After you pass your friend, use your rearview mirrors to see if your friend looks your way.

6 If your friend *does* recognize you, ask what gave you away. Maybe you need to make a more dramatic transformation, or maybe your clothes were so strange that they called attention to you. If your friend *doesn't* recognize you, then call yourself a Super Spy!

MORE FROM HEADQUARTERS

If you want to be even more like Superman, try wearing your quick change outfit *under* your clothes. Just put on some light clothes under a loose-fitting jogging suit. Then all you need is a hiding place (like Superman's phone booth) where you can quickly take off your outer layer. Of course, you'll need to put your outer layer in a bag and carry it with you. That's not what Superman did, but hey, Superman didn't have to worry about getting in trouble with his parents for losing his clothes!

WHAT'S THE SECRET?

Your friend will be on the watch for you in the clothes you were wearing when you last saw each other. Your new look will put you in a completely different category in your friend's eyes, so you should simply blend into the crowd. The more completely you've transformed yourself, the better the chance that your disguise will work. Remember, to make your disguise complete, you've got to believe in it, and act the part completely!

(continued from page 20)

You turn around and see a girl about your age. You quickly answer her question with a firm no and keep walking the way you were going.

"Wait a minute!" she calls after you, but you keep walking.

The next thing you know, you can see in your rearview Spy Shades that you've got two kids tailing behind you.

Trying not to look suspicious, you speed up your walk ever so slightly. You notice that they speed up, too.

Then you quickly turn a corner and find a whole bunch of kids playing on West Carson's rear playground. Perfect! You quickly duck behind the jungle gym and do your quick change, removing your Spy Shades and your jacket and putting on a cap.

You climb to the top of the jungle gym and watch as the two kids who were following you scan the playground, then finally give up. Great work!

But your victory doesn't last long. The next day at school, Holly and Tim tell you that they were called to the principal's office because there were reports that someone from your school had been seen snooping around West Carson's float-building meeting. Holly and Tim had to promise the principal that they wouldn't get involved in any such thing, no matter what they suspected of West Carson. They have to call you off the job.

■ Sorry, but that was a dead end. Turn back and try again.

OPERATION
Straight STORY

So far, you've learned how to look, walk, talk, and act like someone else—but spies don't stop there. A spy might have to take on a whole new *identity*, called a **cover**, and if the cover has to last a while, then the spy will need a **legend**—that is, a whole new life story, with false documents and other paperwork as support. A spy might have to rely on a false identity for as long as a few years, and the longer the identity has to hold up, the more work has to go into creating it and supporting it.

STUFF YOU'LL NEED

- **Pencil and paper**
- **Clothes to match your new identity**
- **Wallet**
- **Magazine photos of people (to serve as your new family), a note addressed to the new you, or anything else the new you might carry**

YOUR NETWORK

- **A friend (or two) to interview the new you**

In this operation, you're going to develop a cover identity for yourself to use on a pretend mission. You'll plan your legend out, and then you'll back it up with **pocket litter** (stuff you carry in your pockets to make your new identity seem real). Then you'll take the "new you" for a test run to see if you can keep your story straight!

WHAT YOU DO

PART 1: CREATE THE NEW YOU

Your first job is to invent your cover identity and legend. Spies choose their cover identities based on what they want to accomplish, so here's your purpose: Pretend that you're going to use this cover identity to secretly **infiltrate** (or sneak into) a rival **spy network** from across town.

1 Using the pencil and paper, answer these questions about the new you. Try to choose an identity that you could easily become and others would easily believe, and make the details easy for you to remember.

2 Now, on the back of the paper, write the life story of the new you. Pretend that you're the new kid in town, and you have to explain to a new acquaintance why you and your family have moved (and from where). Explain what your life has been like up until now—the places you've been and the things that have happened to you. This will help you get to know your character even more.

1. What's your name?

_____

Make the age close to (or the same as) yours.

2. How old are you?

_____

3. Where were you born?

_____

Make sure you have been to these places and can describe them easily.

4. Where else have you lived (and when did you live there)?

PLACES	YEARS

5. Do you speak with an accent? What kind?

_____

Only list languages (and accents) you can actually speak well.

6. What languages do you speak?

_____

7. Who's in your immediate family? List the name, age, and occupation of each person.

NAME	AGE	OCCUPATION

8. Do you have any pets? If so, describe them.

_____

9. Where do you go to school?

_____

10. What are your hobbies and interests?

_____

_____

3. Now choose some clothes for the new you to wear. If you're claiming to be really athletic, you might choose to wear sports clothes. If you're claiming to have come from the countryside, you might wear outdoorsy clothes. It's up to you, but if you want to make sure your wardrobe is realistic down to the last detail, base your clothing choices on your observations of real people.

4 Now it's time to create your pocket litter. So, find a wallet and fill it with some of the following items:

■ Photographs of your new family members (you can clip photos from a magazine for this exercise). For each photo, you should be able to name and describe the "family member" pictured.

■ A note or a letter addressed to the new you.

■ Items, like ticket stubs, sales receipts, or newspaper clippings, from the place you say you're from (if possible).

■ Business cards with your new name on them (which can be made on the Spy University web site (**www.scholastic.com/spy**).

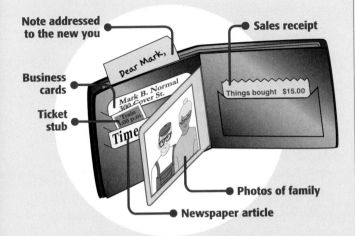

Note addressed to the new you

Business cards

Ticket stub

Sales receipt

Things bought $15.00

Photos of family

Newspaper article

PART 2:
TRY ON THE NEW YOU!

Now you're going to be an actor—you'll actually *become* your new character and perform the role for a friend, so make sure you know your part inside and out!

1 Memorize the legend you outlined in Part 1. Make sure you know all the details of your new identity.

2 Think about the ways the new you should talk, walk, stand, sit, and behave. How will the new you be different from the real you? You don't have to adopt a wildly different manner—maybe just focus on a couple of details, like the way you sit, or the expressions you use when you speak.

3 Dress yourself in the clothes you chose for the new you, and fill your pockets with the pocket litter you created.

4 Invite a friend to come meet the new you. Give your friend the information you wrote in Part 1, and tell your friend to read it carefully,

and be ready to question you about it.

5 Now meet your friend as the new you. You should walk, act, and talk in ways that fit your new identity.

6 Have your friend ask you questions like:

■ Why did you move here?

■ What are your interests?

■ What was your life like before you moved?

■ Where were you born?

■ How many brothers and sisters do you have?

■ What kind of work do your father and mother do?

And so on. Make sure your friend listens carefully to your answers and checks that they match up with your legend.

7 Let your friend look through your wallet and ask you questions about the photos and other items inside. Name and describe each person in your photos, and explain what the other items are.

8 After you're finished, ask your friend how you did. Were you convincing as the new you, or were there times when you didn't keep your story straight? Were there parts of your story that weren't believable? Hopefully not! But if there *were* holes in your legend, you can patch them up and try again with another friend!

MORE FROM HEADQUARTERS

 Do you think you can keep your cover when the pressure's on? Find out on the Spy University web site (**www.scholastic.com/spy**), where you can choose a cover identity, learn your legend, and see if you can correctly answer questions about the new you. Will you keep your story straight, or will you blow your cover? Stop by and see how you do!

WHAT'S THE SECRET?

Was it tough to keep the details of your cover and legend straight? It's not easy, especially if you developed a complicated story. That's why real spies consider it safest to match cover identities as close as possible to real identities. That helps the cover identity hold up under close examination.

Real spies also try to keep their legends as plain and as boring as possible, so they don't attract a lot of interest. No spy wants to have to answer a lot of questions from curious people, like you had to in Part 2!

As for choosing clothing and creating pocket litter—that's a very serious process for spies, especially when they're trying to take on a different nationality. Spies will make sure that the clothes they wear are available in the country they claim to be from, and they'll cut out any labels that might link them to their real home countries. The same goes for hairstyles—spies are careful to make sure that their hairstyles are common in the country they say they're from.

Spies will also get false passports, business cards, calendars, pocket diaries, and other forms of evidence to support their false identities. If a spy claims to be from New York City, she might have in her wallet a sales receipt from a New York department store, a clipping from the *New York Times*, or a ticket stub from a Broadway show. She might even keep a box of matches from a New York restaurant in her pocket. It's this kind of attention to detail that keeps a spy safely undercover!

(continued from page 20)

You turn around and see a girl about your age. She looks sort of familiar, but you're not sure where you know her from. You decide to go with your cover story.

"I go to Greystone School," you say.

"Oh, really?" she says. "What grade are you in?"

You tell her your grade, and she starts rattling off a list of people she knows in your grade at Greystone, asking you if you know any of them. You shrug your shoulders.

"I just moved here," you say.

"But you *must* know Morgan Zellar," she says. "Is *she* in your class?"

You're feeling pressured, so you say yes, you know Morgan.

"Interesting," she says. "Because *I'm* Morgan Zellar, and I definitely don't go to Greystone."

She suddenly grabs your Spy Shades.

"I knew it!" she says. "You *do* go to East Carson! I recognize you from the soccer tournament!"

Just your luck.

Morgan turns and shouts to the float builders, "It's a spy from East Carson!"

Everyone starts shouting, and it's all downhill from there. The teacher in charge takes your name, and the next morning you're called down to your principal's office, along with Tim and Holly, who look at you glumly. No matter how you try to explain that you were only trying to prevent West Carson from spying, it's no use. The principal decides to remove your school's float from the competition this year.

■ Yikes! That was a real nightmare. Better turn back and pick another path!

MOE BERG
A CATCHER AND A SPY

Sometimes a spy's *real* identity is a great cover for spy work. The story of baseball player Moe Berg (1902–1972) is a perfect example.

Berg wasn't your average major-league catcher. Known as "Professor Berg," he was a graduate of Princeton University; he knew about a dozen languages; he had a law degree, and he could speak knowledgeably on a wide range of topics. He was also a very private and secretive person, known among his teammates for quietly disappearing and not offering an explanation when he turned up again. He definitely had the makings of a spy— and that's exactly what he became.

In 1934, while he was traveling in Japan as part of an all-star baseball team that included the legendary Babe Ruth, Berg took the opportunity to make films of Japanese cities, shipyards, factories, and military installations. At the time, relations between Japan and the United States were very tense (the two countries would be at war seven years later), and the Japanese were on high alert for American spies. A foreigner with a movie camera would ordinarily have aroused a lot of suspicion, but Berg, as a celebrity athlete, was able to film throughout his visit without causing alarm.

Eight years later, in 1942, Berg showed his films of Japan to the OSS (Office of Strategic Services), the American foreign intelligence service before the CIA. This was during World War II, when the United States was at war with Japan and needed detailed information to plan bombing raids. It is unclear how useful these films were to the American military, but the OSS thanked Berg enthusiastically for his efforts and later, in 1943, offered him a job as an OSS officer.

Berg had a successful career as a spy for the OSS. During the final years of World War II, he spied in Europe, using his skill with foreign languages to gather information about Germany's progress on its atomic bomb project.

Berg played for a number of major-league baseball teams (including the Chicago White Sox, the Cleveland Indians, and the Boston Red Sox) from 1923 to 1939. He then went on to a successful career as a spy for the United States.

Berg attended Princeton University, where he was a star baseball player.

DRESS for SUCCESS

#11

You've learned how a change of wardrobe can hide your identity, but how else can a spy dress for success? Lots of ways! This operation will show you how to set up a secret **code** with your Spy Signal Pin so your **spy network** will know when you're undercover. You'll also learn how to send signals with shirts, hats, and even your Spy Shades. That way, when you have something to say, you can say it in style!

STUFF YOU'LL NEED

- 👓 Spy Signal Pin
- Shirts of various colors
- 👓 Spy Shades
- Cap or hats of different colors

YOUR NETWORK

- Some friends to watch what you wear

WHAT YOU DO

PART 1: SAFETY PIN

Let's imagine you're undercover, and you see a member of your spy network across a crowded room. It would blow your cover if your fellow spy approached you and addressed you by your real name. How can you prevent that? Use your Spy Signal Pin! Its eyes can be three different colors, and each one can send a different signal to your spy network.

1 Look at the back of your Spy Signal Pin, and you'll see a wheel of colors behind each eye.

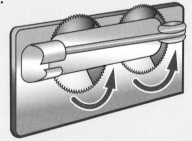

Turn the wheels, and watch the colors of the eyes change.

2 Meet with your spy network to agree on what each color means. For example, red eyes could mean you're under-cover, and you can't be approached at all. Yellow eyes could mean that you can be approached, but only when no one else is around. Green eyes could mean that you can be freely approached at any time, since your status is not operational.

Meet at the park next Saturday at noon.	Expect an invisible ink message in your mail.	Ready to load dead drop.	I am under surveillance. Don't approach.

3 Test out your Spy Signal Pin. Pin it on your shirt (or on your lapel if you're a snazzy, jacket-wearing spy), and set the color to red. See if your friends keep their distance like they're supposed to! Try other settings and see if your friends respond correctly.

PART 2: CLOTHING CODE

Ready to wear more messages? Then follow these steps to learn how to encode your wardrobe!

1 Meet with your spy network to establish your clothing code (see above). For example, you might decide that if you wear a red shirt, it means that you want to have a meeting in the park the next Saturday at noon. Or, if you wear a green-striped shirt, it could mean that you have information ready to exchange at a certain **dead drop** location at a preset time. You could also attach meaning to a hat, to your Spy Shades, or even to something you carry.

2 You and your spy network should learn your clothing code and plan to see each other on a daily basis.

3 Take your signals for a test run! Wear a red shirt one day, and see how many members of your spy network meet you in the park the next Saturday at noon!

MORE FROM HEADQUARTERS

Think of more ways your clothing can be coded. If you normally wear your watch on your left arm, wearing it on your right arm could be a signal of some sort. In the winter, your clothing code can be built around the colors of your scarves, hats, and gloves. Be creative! You could even attach meanings to different hairstyles!

WHAT'S THE SECRET?

Your Spy Signal Pin gives you an easy way to alert your spy network that you're on an undercover operation. It's great for situations when you can't be seen talking to other spies or acting like the real you. Try to find a place on your coat or shirt to wear your pin so it's visible, but won't attract a lot of attention from non-spies. If someone asks you about

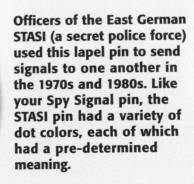

Officers of the East German STASI (a secret police force) used this lapel pin to send signals to one another in the 1970s and 1980s. Like your Spy Signal pin, the STASI pin had a variety of dot colors, each of which had a pre-determined meaning.

your cool pin, make sure you have a story to explain why you're wearing it (say your grandpa gave it to you or something)!

As for your clothing code, that's really easy to hide, since it's not likely that anyone outside your spy network will realize that your shirt has a special meaning. Just make sure that you only encode a few items from your wardrobe. Otherwise, you'll have nothing to wear that

doesn't send some kind of signal!

Remember also that the key to this code is that the person who's supposed to receive your messages sees you on a regular basis. If the person can't see you every day, at least make sure that there's one day each week when you'll definitely see each other. That's the day you'll wear your code!

(continued from page 31)

You follow behind the old lady, keeping a good distance away, until you see a group of kids approach her, then stop to *talk* with her! You recognize the kids from West Carson's float-building meeting! You're afraid they might notice you any second, so you quietly snap a picture, then turn around and slip away.

The next day, you arrive early at the float-building meeting, hoping the old lady will show up so you can catch her in the act. You've brought your camera, and you're wearing your best running shoes. This is the big day! And sure enough, you don't have to wait long before she arrives. You wait till she turns to go, and you call to Tim and Holly.

"Come with me," you say. "I've found the West Carson spy."

You sneak up behind the old lady and grab her wig. Sure enough, she's really a boy!

"Hey!" he shouts, trying to run away, but you, Tim, and Holly grab hold of him.

"Are you from West Carson?" Tim asks.

"What's your name?" Holly demands.

"I'm not saying anything!" the boy says.

"You don't have to," you say, pulling out your camera and snapping a picture. "Pictures say a thousand words."

"Hey," the boy shouts, trying to grab the camera, but you quickly move away while Holly and Tim hold him back.

"You were busted anyway," you say. "I followed you back to West Carson yesterday, and I watched you report back to the float builders."

Tim calls Mr. Zinno, one of the teachers who's helping with the float, and you fill him in on the whole story.

"I can't believe it," Mr. Zinno says. "A spy? Why would you even bother? It's just a parade—it's supposed to be fun!"

"It's fun if you *win*," the boy says.

"Why can't you win with your own ideas?" Holly asks.

"Or are you just too dumb to *have* any ideas?" Tim asks.

"We have ideas," the boy says. "And we're *way* smarter than you. We know you guys are the only real competition in the school category—so we figured that the easiest way to win was to do exactly what you guys did, but better."

"Oh, *my*," Mr. Zinno says. "I can't believe I'm hearing this!"

It's a shocker, but it's true. Mr. Zinno takes the news straight to the principal, and by lunchtime the next day, the word is out: West Carson has been forced to withdraw its float from the parade. Tim and Holly can't thank you enough for catching that spy in disguise!

■ Congratulations!
Quest accomplished!

Yes!

Escape FROM IRAN

This is the story of a great escape, made possible by some clever **covers**, **legends**, and **disguises**. It's the story of six Americans who got stuck in Iran at an unfortunate time, and a CIA officer, a master of disguise, who found a way to get them out.

In 1979, there was a revolution in Iran in which a government supported by the United States was overthrown. A strong anti-American feeling developed in the country under its new leadership. The Iranians suspected that Americans were spying on them, and that the American embassy in Tehran was nothing but a den of spies. Suspicions grew and grew until finally, in November 1979, hundreds of young Iranians stormed the American embassy compound, taking about seventy Americans hostage.

But six American diplomats managed to escape. They were working in a building toward the back of the embassy compound, and a sudden rainstorm provided the distraction they needed to sneak away unnoticed. They took refuge in the Canadian embassy, but they knew they would not be safe there for long. Since the Iranian government was supporting the embassy takeover, it was clear that Iran was not a safe place for Americans. The six diplomats needed to get out of Iran. And fast.

So Antonio Mendez was called in. Mendez was a CIA disguise expert who had successfully handled many **exfiltration** operations (that is, operations where people had to be helped out of dangerous situations). He was also highly skilled at developing cover identities and legends to support them, having spent years in the CIA's Technical Services Division, where he handcrafted fake passports, ID cards, and other kinds of official documents.

Getting the six Americans out of Iran posed a huge challenge. What kind of cover story would explain what six Americans, four men and two women, ranging in age from twenty-seven to fifty-four, were doing in Iran? Would an Iranian passport control officer immediately guess that the six were really diplomats and detain them as suspected spies? The risk was especially high, since three of the six were high-level embassy employees who would be very recognizable to Iranian officials.

After much consideration, Mendez and his colleagues settled upon a plan. The first step was to shed the six of their American identities. Through a special arrangement with the Canadian government, the six were given Canadian passports. Then, Mendez came up with a possible cover story: The six would be Canadian filmmakers, visiting Iran to scout out locations for their next film.

With help from contacts in Hollywood, Mendez determined what jobs each of the six individuals might hold on a film production team, from writer to cameraman to production manager. He established his movie production company, Studio Six Productions (named for the six diplomats), by renting office space on a Hollywood studio lot, setting up a telephone number, and even renting furniture. He then found a suitable script for the movie, which he titled *Argo*, and took out two full-page ads in major Hollywood magazines to announce its upcoming production. He developed an **alias** (or false name) for himself, Kevin Costa Harkins, and got himself Studio Six business cards in that name. Finally, before leaving for Iran, Mendez stocked up on Hollywood pocket litter, including a matchbook from a Hollywood restaurant.

When he arrived in Iran, Mendez secretly met the six. They were getting very nervous and were anxious to hear how Mendez planned to help them escape. They listened as Mendez described the film company option as well as a backup cover he'd planned (in which the six were traveling teachers). The six considered their options and decided: The film company it would be.

Now it was time to prepare the six for their speedy exit. Mendez helped the diplomats disguise their appearances and personalities by changing their clothing and hairstyles to fit their new occupations. Then he made sure that each of the six went through a practice **interrogation**, in which a Canadian embassy employee, pretending to be an Iranian official, shouted at them and tried to get them to slip up and break their covers.

A button thanking Canada for its help in the rescue

A newspaper article on the rescue

A photo of the six after their rescue

The business card Mendez used to support his cover identity, Kevin Costa Harkins

A boarding pass for the flight to Switzerland (where the six flew to safety)

A collection of items relating to the rescue of the six Americans from Iran.

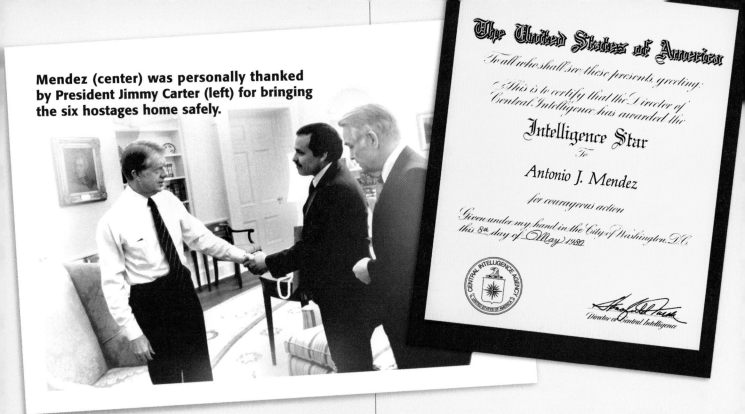

Mendez (center) was personally thanked by President Jimmy Carter (left) for bringing the six hostages home safely.

The United States of America

To all who shall see these presents, greeting:

This is to certify that the Director of Central Intelligence has awarded the

Intelligence Star

To

Antonio J. Mendez

for courageous action

Given under my hand in the City of Washington, D.C. this 8th day of May 1980.

Director of Central Intelligence

The next morning, the six went to the airport. One by one, they made it through passport control with their mocked-up passports and paperwork, and after a tense wait for a delayed flight, they were safely on their way to Switzerland. Mission accomplished!

On May 8, 1980, Mendez received an Intelligence Star, the CIA's second-highest award, for his success in this operation. The award ceremony was kept quiet, though, because most of the other embassy employees were still being held hostage in Tehran. In fact, fifty-two of them remained in captivity for 444 days, until their release was finally negotiated with the Iranian government.

For many years after the escape, the credit for the rescue of the six went to the Canadian government. It wasn't until Mendez published his memoir, *The Master of Disguise*, in 1999, that the whole story was finally uncovered.

To celebrate its fiftieth anniversary in 1997, the CIA honored fifty of its most distinguished officers with Trailblazer Awards. Antonio Mendez was among them. He is shown here (on the left) receiving his Trailblazer Award from George J. Tenet, the CIA director.

catch you later!

Now that you're familiar with your disguise options, you can choose your disguises wisely, to suit your goals—whether your goal is to quickly escape from a sticky situation or to secretly watch what's going on at a rival school (like you did in your Spy Quest!). That's the key to the art of disguise: creating a disguise or a cover that suits your purpose well.

Here's a final challenge to cap off your disguise training. You've worked a lot on *creating* disguises, but what about seeing *through* disguises? For a quick test of your skills, have a look at these photos of people in disguise. Each person is shown twice, once for real, and once in disguise. Can you match the two photos of the same person?

A

B

C

D

E

F

You can check your answers in the Answer Spot below. We'll see you next month!

the answer spot

Page 48 (Catch You Later!):

A (real) and **D** (disguise) are both images of the same unidentified spy.

B (real) and **F** (disguise) are both images of "Wild Bill"

Donovan, the director of the OSS (Office of Strategic Services), the forerunner of the CIA, from 1942 to 1945. **E** (real) and **C** (disguise) are both images of

H. Keith Melton, one of your Spy University instructors! The disguise he's wearing was created by Antonio Mendez, whom you met in this month's Spy Feature.

48